Listen to
Your Kitten Purr

Listen to Your Kitten Purr

by Lilo Hess

Charles Scribner's Sons   New York

Copyright © 1980 Lilo Hess

Library of Congress Cataloging in Publication Data
Hess, Lilo.
Listen to your kitten purr.
SUMMARY: After they are mistreated and abandoned by their first owners,
Mindy and her kittens find good homes.
1. Cats—Legend and stories.   [1. Cats]
I. Title.
SF445.7.H47   636.8′08′87   79-19531
ISBN 0-684-16428-0

1 3 5 7 9 11 13 15 17 19 MD/C 20 18 16 14 12 10 8 6 4 2

It was early one morning in September. The white mist was just rising from a small pond and the adjoining green hills of a golf course when two men walked by the pond. They were golfers searching for a lost ball. They noticed a brown bundle floating in the water not far from the bank. They had almost passed it, when they heard a noise and thought they saw the bundle move. Startled, they came closer to investigate it. The mud on the bank of the pond was so soft that they sank in up to their ankles but could not reach the bundle. It was a sack made of burlap, and something in it wiggled and squirmed and made frantic cries. Since the men could not find a pole or stick long enough to pull it in, they rushed to the nearest telephone and called the local agent of the Society for the Prevention of Cruelty to Animals.

The agent arrived quickly at the scene, equipped with a long pole, a cage, and dry towels. This was not the first time he had to rescue little animals from cruel acts of uncaring people.

The pole had metal prongs at the end, and the agent pulled the sack toward the bank slowly and carefully so as not to injure the animals inside.

When the sack was opened five little kittens emerged and scampered off in all directions. They were wet, shivering, and frightened, but they were unharmed because the sack had not been weighted down with rocks or other heavy objects to keep it underwater, and the loose weave of the burlap had let enough air inside for the kittens to breathe.

After the kittens were dried, they were taken to the animal shelter. There they were placed in a cage and given warm milk. Soon the exhausted kittens fell asleep all curled up close together. Within a few days all five kittens were adopted.

They were the lucky ones, since most abandoned animals do not find new homes. How did the little cats get into such a predicament?

It all started about nine months before with some other kittens. Those kittens were born on a farm and led a good life. They and some older cats were well fed and allowed to sleep in the house on cold nights. During the day they ran and played in the farmyard, the barns, or the adjoining fields.

When they were about six months old, a strange thing happened on the farm. A young deer, a buck, started to visit them. He came out of the woods and watched the young cats. First he was a bit timid and kept his distance, but soon he came closer and closer and finally sniffed and licked them. The cats pressed against the deer and seemed to enjoy his company. The farmer and his family watched all this with amazement. When they noticed that the young buck licked out the almost empty cat food dish, they put out extra food. The deer enjoyed the cat food, cleaning up the dish and looking for more.

The young buck appeared now every morning and every evening to take his meal with the cats. They all ate out of the same dish, and when they had finished, the deer licked every cat in turn. Then he played tag with them, running all over the farmyard and in and out of the barns. Before dark the deer started back into his woods. Some of the cats accompanied him a little way through the fields and then returned home. At daybreak they waited for him at the barn. This strange friendship was reported in the local newspaper, and soon people came to the farm to watch Cricket, as the farmer's children had named the deer, frolicking with the young cats.

Two visiting children and their parents wanted to own one of the "famous" cats, and the farmer agreed to let them pick one. The children had a hard time deciding which of the cute cats they should pick. Finally they decided on a small female tabby, or tiger-striped cat.

The name "tabby" is supposed to date far back in history. In the city of Baghdad in Iraq is a district called Attabiah. There silk goods were manufactured that resembled the patterns and shadings of the short-haired local tiger cats. This silk was very popular in Europe and sold under the trade name of Tabbi silk.

The children were delighted with their new pet and named her Mindy. But Mindy's new family had never owned a cat before and did not know how to care for it or what to feed it. They thought that milk and bread were all a cat ever needed. Mindy, like many other cats that are almost mature, did not care for milk anymore. She had been used to a cat food diet consisting of one-third canned or semimoist food and two thirds dry food. She sat in front of her dish of milk and stared at it, then she walked around it and made scratching motions as if she wanted to bury it. Finally she walked away from it.

The children never thought that animals had feelings and moods and that they needed to have some privacy. They played with Mindy all the time. They carried her about, dressed her up in dolls' clothes, tickled her, and pulled her whiskers. Mindy became very upset and frightened and defended herself with her sharp claws.

Cat's claws are retractable. When not in use they are kept in a fold of skin called a sheath. But they can be extended with lightning speed and are a formidable weapon.

When Mindy scratched the children, they screamed and punished her by hitting her. Mindy avoided the rough-playing children by hiding under furniture or in closets. On the second day the children had already lost interest in the little cat and hardly gave her a glance.

Mindy longed to go outdoors. She stared out of the window and cried until the children's mother opened the door for her.

Outside, Mindy immediately set out to find food. She was very hungry. The easiest way to find something to eat was to raid the neighbors' garbage cans. She also found crusts of bread and bits of cake that playing children had dropped. Mindy chewed on grasses and ate bits of dandelions. She caught some crickets and butterflies. She had never been an accomplished hunter, but now she had to learn quickly to survive.

In typical cat fashion, Mindy sat motionless under a bush or in the tall grass. When she spotted a likely prey, she fixed her eyes on it and crawled closer, making her body as flat as possible. Then she drew herself up and pounced. Sometimes she was lucky and caught a mouse or other small rodent.

Mindy stayed outside day and night. She rested in the grass or under bushes. On rainy or stormy nights she crawled into a garage or a workshop or under someone's porch.

After about five or six days, Mindy went home again for a short visit. Mindy was not abused or played with anymore—she was just ignored. After a few hours, she slipped outside again when the door was opened. No one paid any attention to her comings and goings.

It was inevitable that Mindy would meet other cats outside. With some she fought, and loud yowling could be heard at night. With some she made friends. A black and white tomcat appeared and pursued Mindy for several days. At first she was afraid of him, but he licked her reassuringly and possessively. They mated, and a day later the tomcat disappeared as suddenly as he had come.

Mindy was pregnant. The first five weeks showed no change in her, but in the sixth week her body began to swell and she became lazy. When she was seven weeks pregnant it was difficult for her to chase mice, and the leftovers in garbage cans were not enough to sustain her. She spent most of her time dozing in the morning sun. When it got too hot, she sought out shady bushes. She was always hungry.

In her eighth week, she returned to the house. Once inside, she searched restlessly for a comfortable place to have her babies. She tried the sofa, the kitchen cupboard, and even the fireplace, but nothing suited her. She meowed so loudly and so persistently that the family noticed her strange behavior and her swollen abdomen.

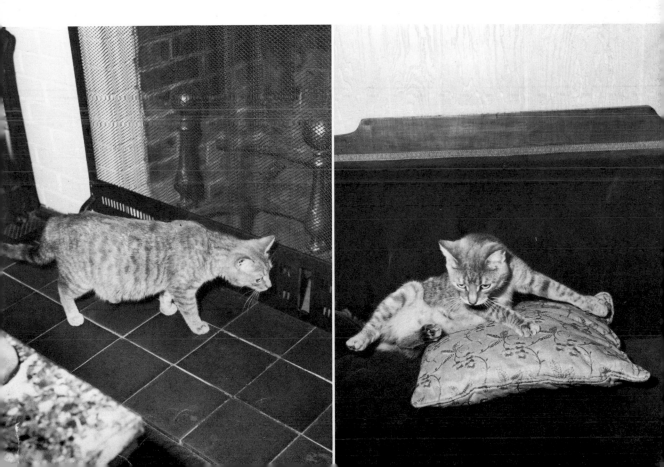

Everyone was delighted at the prospect of having kittens in the house. The children were looking forward to playing with the kittens, and their parents figured that the kittens could be sold. Once again Mindy was the center of attention.

A box lined with newspaper was placed in a quiet corner near the kitchen, and Mindy seemed to like it. She spent several hours sleeping or just sitting in it. She was also given some table scraps to eat as well as a bowl of milk. This time she drank all the milk and asked for more.

Three days after she had come into the house, Mindy got ready for the birth of her kittens. She stretched out in her box and cleaned herself. She paid special attention to her stomach area, her nipples, and her tail. A cat's tongue is covered with tiny hooks that make a very effective cleaning device.

Mindy was just about to fall asleep, when the contractions started. A few minutes later the first kitten slid out quickly and seemingly without discomfort to Mindy.

The baby was encased in a transparent membrane and attached by the umbilical cord to an organ called the placenta.

Although Mindy had never given birth before, she knew instinctively what to do. She quickly tore the membrane and licked the kitten's face, mouth, and nostrils in order to remove any mucus and stimulate the baby to breathe. Then she cleaned the rest of its body and cut the umbilical cord by chewing it off about two inches from the kitten's stomach. The little piece left on the body would dry up and fall off in a few days. After the cord had been cut, Mindy ate the placenta, as if she knew that the vitamins and minerals in this organ were good for her.

She rolled the little wet baby over and back and forth until it became lively and pushed itself toward its mother's nipples to get its first meal. But before it could get a good hold on the nipple and suckle, Mindy strained her body, and the second kitten arrived. Mindy worked quickly; she had hardly time to clean up one kitten before the next one appeared. After the fifth kitten had been cleaned, she relaxed and lay exhausted on the blood-stained paper. No more kittens were coming.

The children, who had been watching the birth, removed the paper and put a piece of dry, clean carpeting into the box. They also brought a dish of cat food and fresh milk to Mindy. Mindy immediately ate all the food and drank all the milk, and then settled down in the box, curling her body carefully around her babies.

All the babies nursed hungrily and then fell asleep, their tiny mouths still holding tight to the nipples.

The first few days of the kittens' life passed very quietly. They slept and nursed, and from time to time they crawled and pushed a little. If the children picked them up, they wailed loudly. Mindy stayed with them almost all the time and kept them warm and clean.

The eyes and ears of the babies were firmly closed at birth but started to open just a little by the tenth day. On the twelfth day the eyes were fully open and the kittens could also hear. They became increasingly lively and started to crawl in and out of the box.

The family still treated Mindy well and gave her enough food so that she could produce milk for her babies. Mindy seemed content. Like other cats, she could express her feelings and emotions through body language. A tail carried high and straight up has been interpreted to mean that the cat is happy about something. Horizontal lashing of the tail with ears laid

back is supposed to show anger and annoyance. The cat's paws may slap a person or another animal in anger, or gently pat with affection. Kneading means ecstasy. Cats lick each other or their owners to demonstrate love, or as reassurance when they are nervous. Whiskers can be extended when a cat is investigating new surroundings, they can hang down listlessly when a cat is sick, or they can twitch to show excitement. Purring and even drooling mean great contentment and a sense of being at ease.

Mindy's human family was not interested in her feelings. They only wanted her to take care of the kittens so that they would grow quickly and could be sold soon. At the age of three weeks the kittens did not want to stay in the box anymore. They were especially attracted to anything soft, such as rugs or pillows, and they loved to crawl into the laundry basket or hide in the linen closet.

In one of the closets was an old woven dog basket with a soft, bouncy mattress that the kittens liked and jumped into every chance they had, so the children substituted this for the box. Now the kittens did not wander away so often, because they could see what went on in the house through the open weave. They also had fun climbing over, through, and around the basket. A kitten inside the basket could stick its little paw out and bat at a sister or brother that was playing on the outside. The soft mattress was great for rolling and bouncing up and down.

At the age of four weeks the kittens could drink milk from a saucer, and Mindy showed them how to use a litter box. Kittens learn mostly from their mother or from each other.

Kittens are naturally curious and investigate everything. Mindy often disciplined them with a swat if she did not like what they were doing. She cuffed the babies for climbing a scratching post that she herself wanted to use at the moment. She disciplined them for chasing the broom or hitching a ride on it when the room was swept. But the kittens never seemed to be upset by their mother's interference. They just invented other games.

At five weeks the kittens became a great nuisance to every-one. They climbed up and down the new sofa in the living room. They played hide and seek under the furniture, bump-ing into things and often knocking something over. The day they found a ball of knitting yarn they enjoyed themselves tre-mendously. They chased it, pushed it, pounced on it, chewed it, and got completely entangled in it. When the children's mother saw it, she spanked the kittens in anger, but they had already forgotten about it and probably did not know why they were being punished. They just looked surprised and washed their faces. The family decided that the kittens must be sold imme-diately.

All the kittens were put into a basket and set on a table in front of the house. A sign was put up offering the kittens for sale at five dollars each. The children took turns watching the kittens and pushing them back into the basket when they climbed out. A few people stopped by, petted the kittens, and said how cute they were, but no one wanted to buy one. The next day the price was reduced to two-fifty, later to one dollar, and finally to twenty-five cents. But no one wanted them, even when a new sign announced that the kittens were free.

The family had also placed an ad in the local newspaper, but the pet column already had many listings for free kittens and puppies, and there was no response. The family got very upset because they did not know what to do with the kittens, which played more wildly and ate more food every day.

It was then that they decided to drown the kittens. In their haste to be done with the unpleasant job, they even forgot to weigh the burlap bag down with something heavy to keep it underwater. This is why the little kittens had survived.

Mindy missed her kittens at first and cried for them, but after two days she seemed to have forgotten about them. The family stopped giving her food and attention, and she was put out of the house again to hunt for her food or go hungry.

As it had been her way before the kittens were born, Mindy stayed outdoors for a week or two and then returned to the house for a short visit.

When she returned this time, everything was different. People were rushing about, big boxes were filled with household belongings, closets were bare. Mindy walked about aimlessly, went in and out of the closets, or jumped on top of the boxes until someone grabbed her and put her outdoors again.

A few days later a big van came, and men loaded all the boxes and the furniture in it. Mindy was sitting on the door-steps in the afternoon sun, licking and cleaning her fur, when the family emerged and, without a glance at the little cat, got into the car and drove away. Mindy did not know it, but she had been abandoned.

Mindy continued her now familiar vagabond life, hunting or scrounging for food. Sometimes neighbors were annoyed by her scratching in their flower beds or vegetable gardens, or when yowling or fighting cats disturbed their sleep at night. From time to time Mindy got a good meal when kind people set out a dish of leftovers for the homeless cats.

The sunny days of autumn became fewer and the nights were already very cold. Mindy did not like to sleep in the open anymore and returned to her old home.

Mindy looked thin, and despite her efforts to clean herself, her fur looked dull and dirty and she had picked up fleas. She sat patiently in front of the door and meowed softly. The door was opened and Mindy entered. She was greeted with a cry of joy by a strange young girl who scooped her up in her arms and seemed delighted to see her. The unfamiliar smells and new people made Mindy shy and skittish. Her fur stood straight up, her ears lay flat back against her head, and her whiskers twitched. But the girl stroked her and talked gently to her and so did her brother and her parents, who had gathered around to greet the new arrival.

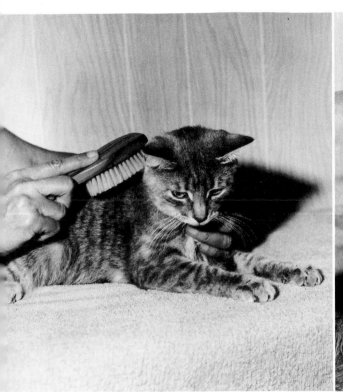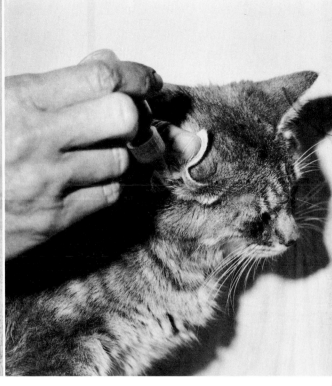

After Mindy had relaxed a little and inspected the new objects in the familiar house, she was given food and water. Later that day she got a litter box and the girl brushed the dirt and the sticky burrs out of her fur. This was a new experience for Mindy, and she seemed to enjoy it. But when the girl cleaned the cat's ears with a cotton swab and then put drops in them to rid them of mites, Mindy protested and extended her claws and scratched the girl. Then she fled and hid behind a big chair.

The new occupants of the house had found the old wicker dog basket the former tenants had left behind, and they got it out now and cleaned it up for Mindy. They were delighted when the little tabby went in it right away and stretched out and went to sleep in it. They did not know that Mindy had already spent many contented hours with her kittens in the same basket.

The next morning Mindy greeted her new friends by rubbing her back against their legs and purring loudly. The girl fed her, played with her awhile, and later brushed her again and put a flea collar on her.

After about a week, Mindy's thin body had filled out and her fur was again sleek and shiny. She spent most of the time in the house and went outdoors only for a few hours of fresh air when it was not too cold.

Then one day Mindy was gathered up and put in a small dark box. She was very frightened and meowed loudly. She was taken to a veterinarian.

Her new owners liked her so much that they had decided to keep her, but they did not want her to have kittens. They knew about the hundreds of thousands of homeless and unwanted cats, kittens, and dogs that roam the streets, parks, and alleys, starving and breeding in an endless chain. They felt responsible for their pet and had decided that Mindy should be "spayed." This simple operation prevents the female animal from getting pregnant. A male animal can be "altered" to prevent him from fertilizing a female. It does not change an animal's character, nor does it cause him or her to be fat and lazy, as some people think.

The young girl felt very nervous about her pet's operation, but the vet explained it to her step by step.

After a thorough checkup, Mindy would be given an injection to anesthetize her. Within minutes she would be asleep and relaxed, breathing regularly. Mindy would be stretched out on her back on the operating table, her feet tied with a loose knot so that she could not curl up the way sleeping cats like to do. Her abdomen would be shaved, and a mask would be put over her face. The mask would be connected to a machine that could dispense oxygen or anesthesia as it was needed.

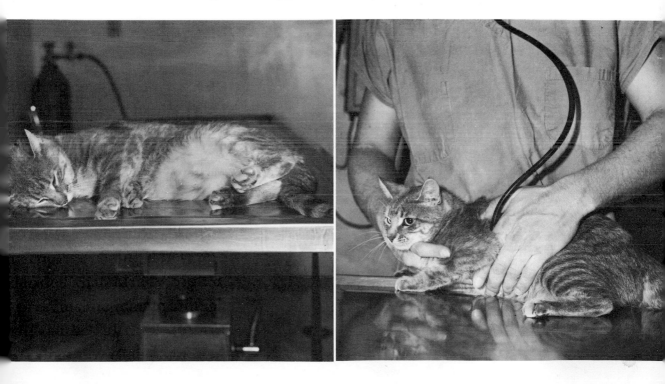

Just like a surgeon operating on a human patient, the vet would scrub before putting on the surgical gloves. The cat's shaved abdomen would then be disinfected and covered with a sterile pad. The pad had a slit in its center just where the three-inch incision would be made. Clamps held the incision open so that the long, thin uterus and the ovaries could be lifted out and snipped off. The wound would then be disinfected, closed with a few stitches, and disinfected again.

The operation over, the sleeping animal would be taken to a warm, quiet cage to recover. Because Mindy would be sleepy and groggy for several hours, the vet suggested that she remain at the animal hospital over night.

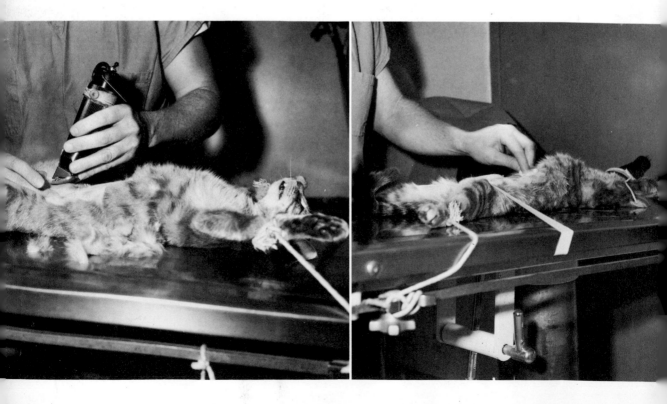

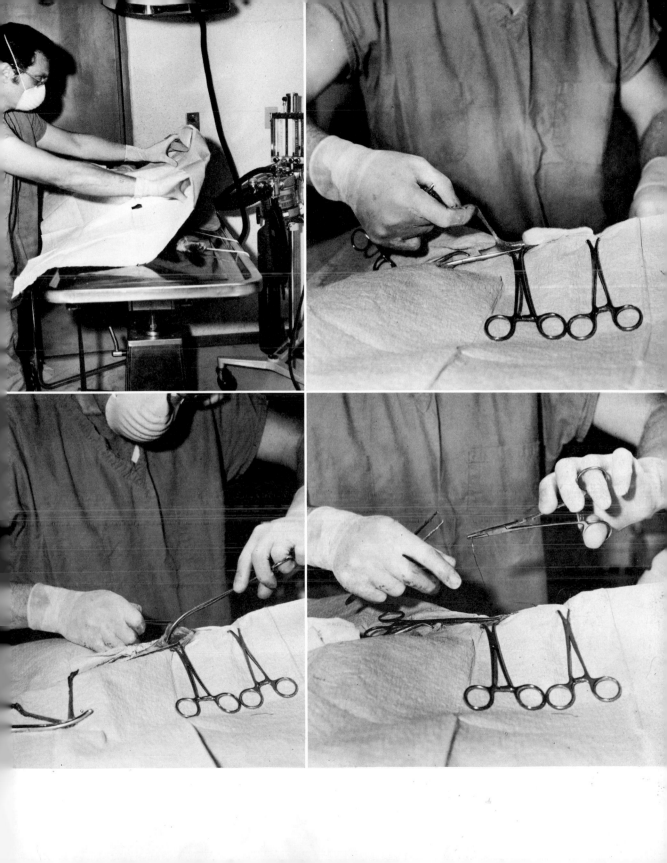

The young girl felt reassured, but not until she picked up her pet the following day and saw that Mindy was really fine did she stop worrying.

Mindy recovered quickly. She was given good food, extra vitamins, and plenty of rest in her wicker basket. After ten days the vet removed the stitches and Mindy ran and played as before. The fur would grow back over the shaved area in a few weeks.

Since no one in her new family knew her name, Mindy was now called Annie—for Orphan Annie. She got used to her name quickly, just as she had gotten used to the good food, the brushing, and the kind treatment she now received. She rewarded her owners with the affection, the companionship, and the loud, happy purrs of a well-loved pet.